YOUR KNOWLEDGE HAS VALUE

- We will publish your bachelor's and
  master's thesis, essays and papers

- Your own eBook and book -
  sold worldwide in all relevant shops

- Earn money with each sale

Upload your text at www.GRIN.com
and publish for free

Bibliographic information published by the German National Library:

The German National Library lists this publication in the National Bibliography; detailed bibliographic data are available on the Internet at http://dnb.dnb.de .

This book is copyright material and must not be copied, reproduced, transferred, distributed, leased, licensed or publicly performed or used in any way except as specifically permitted in writing by the publishers, as allowed under the terms and conditions under which it was purchased or as strictly permitted by applicable copyright law. Any unauthorized distribution or use of this text may be a direct infringement of the author s and publisher s rights and those responsible may be liable in law accordingly.

Imprint:

Copyright © 2018 GRIN Verlag
Print and binding: Books on Demand GmbH, Norderstedt Germany
ISBN: 9783668739710

This book at GRIN:

https://www.grin.com/document/430943

Elvira Tafarrohi

The Groucho-Effect. Are consumers really confused or do they just not care enough?

An experimental approach

GRIN Verlag

GRIN - Your knowledge has value

Since its foundation in 1998, GRIN has specialized in publishing academic texts by students, college teachers and other academics as e-book and printed book. The website www.grin.com is an ideal platform for presenting term papers, final papers, scientific essays, dissertations and specialist books.

Visit us on the internet:

http://www.grin.com/

http://www.facebook.com/grincom

http://www.twitter.com/grin_com

Inhaltsverzeichnis

1. Introduction 2
2. Theoretical background 2
3. The experiment 4
   - 3.1. Part 1 4
   - 3.2. Part 2 5
   - 3.3. Part 3 5
   - 3.4. The socio-demographic questionnaire 6
4. Data/ results 6
5. Conclusion/ Further research 7
6. Sources/ Literature 8

Are consumers really confused or do they just not care enough? An experimental approach.

1. Introduction

Whenever you open a newspaper there might be an article about global warming, about critically endangered animal species, or air pollution and the health consequences. Those articles should be like a wake-up call to finally change peoples' behaviour and save the environment, and lastly ourselves. Then you go to the supermarket and you see normal products and some products claiming to be "green", "eco-friendly", "fair" or "produced responsible" others with labels on it to prove it. What those labels really prove is often not clear to the consumers. This is when we speak about *label credence goods*. Even after consuming a certain labelled product the consumer cannot be sure about its quality and the applied standards. Thus, consumers must form believes about the quality of the product and the credibility of the label. One paper analyses this behaviour theoretically, namely "Label Confusion: The Groucho Effect of Uncertain Standards" written by Rick Harbaugh, John Maxwell and Beatrice Roussillon in 2011. There, the authors focus on ecolabels for environmental quality. As labels are used as a sign for certain quality, having a label should increase the value of a product. The largest effect should be for products when consumers assume it is of a bad quality. The authors claim that this is not working simple like that if the applied standard of the label is unknown by the consumer. In this case, consumers indeed will update their believes but not only about the product in a positive direction but also for the label in a bad direction. The purpose of this paper is to test some of the hypotheses and assumption of the Groucho-paper to shed some light on what consumers really think and if labels increase the perceived quality of a product and, thus, increase the willingness to pay of consumers.

2. Theoretical background

The hypotheses we test experimentally are inspired by the work of Harbaugh and colleagues. The main difference compared to other literature is that they do not assume that labelling standards are common knowledge among consumers. Their assumption is that consumers have a prior distribution of labelling standards, which can be precise, diffuse, skewed or something else, meaning that consumers might have a clue if a label is more of a higher or of lower standard. Every consumer has a prior belief about the product and about the label. This results in basically four different combinations of product quality and label standard. Either a consumer has a positive opinion about the product and, at the same time, has a positive opinion about the labelling standard or has a negative belief about both. Then, those believes match and the consumers opinion about both, the label and the product, is reinforced. There is no updating of believes necessary or the update could just be that the consumer now is convinced that the product fulfils a high standard. It is less straightforward if the believes do not match. It could be that the consumer has a positive opinion about the product but assumes the label to be a low standard label. This might decrease the value of the product or it might not have any influence on your opinion at all. The fourth case is a negative opinion about the product combined with a (assumed) high standard label. Two things can happen, either the reputation of the product and the perceived quality is increased by the label or the bad reputation of the product decreases the reputation of the label. The first effect is the desired effect by companies when it comes to labelling. A label should be an indicator of good quality what becomes even more important if the prior belief about the product is bad. But if the applied standard of a label is unknown by consumers or a product has a very low reputation people infer that the label should be of a weak standard, so they decrease the reputation of the label. This means that "the incentive for labelling is undermined when the problem of information asymmetry, and hence the potential gain from labelling, is the greatest."[1] This (negative) effect is named "Groucho-effect" after the US-American actor Groucho Marx (1890-1977) who once said: "I refuse to join any club that would have me for a member."[2] The paper's approach is very theoretical but with a relatable intuition behind it. The less a consumer knows about the product and the applied label standard the smaller is the informativeness of the label and the more confused is the consumer about the real environmental quality of the product.

We test a few hypotheses in our experiment. Harbaugh and colleagues write that the existence of multiple labels with different applied standard should decrease information asymmetries theoretically and consumers should be more informed the finer the evaluation system is. But they argue that if consumers do not know the standard of a label they will only infer that the label just shows that the product has met the easiest of all standards. In their model the probability of a product being of the very lowest

---

[1] Harbaugh et al. (2011), p.1513
[2] https://www.focus.de/kultur/vermischtes/groucho-marx-zum-40-todestag-die-besten-sprueche-von-groucho-marx_id_7490209.html

standard is an action with zero probability and consumers will not expect it anyway. To test this hypothesis, we will show participants in the first part of the experiment different pictures of products and ask them to estimate the environmental quality of them. The baseline is generated by showing products without any label. We have two additional treatments, one is showing the product with a real label on it and the other is showing the product with a fake label. In the second part participants are asked to state their believes about the applied standards of the labels we are showing them. Again, we present existing labels and phantasy labels. The third part of the experiment is to test whether consumers expect products to be labelled and if they have a higher willingness to pay for labelled products. When they reach the last task of this part, we offer them to claim information about the labels. This shows, whether participants are interested in knowing more about labels or not. The last part is a questionnaire, where we ask for socio-demographic information of the participants. This helps us to find potential differences between groups or gender differences.

3. The experiment

As explained above, this approach consists of three experimental tasks and a questionnaire in the end. Participants are students from the University Innsbruck. The experiment takes place in the research lab in the SoWi building. Each participant is asked to answer all four parts. The experiment will take 50 to 60 minutes. The show-up fee is 8€ and paid to all participants after completing the last task, the questionnaire.

3.1. Part 1

In the first part of the experiment we show different pictures of products to our participants. Then we ask them to estimate the environmental quality of them on a scale from zero (*not environmental friendly at all*) to 100 (*absolutely environmental friendly*). The baseline is generated by showing products without any label. We have two additional treatments, one is showing the product with a real label on it and the other is showing the product with a fake label. In this part, we use the between-design. This means that each participant is shown only one version of the same product. This is because we do not want to make the real intention and topic too obvious. Each participant should evaluate the environmental quality of 9 different products, including three pictures without a label (baseline), three pictures with the true label (treatment 1) and three pictures with a phantasy label (treatment 2). We included the answer "I don't know the product." for the case that the shown product is unknown for the participant. Then, another picture of the same treatment is shown.

3.2. Part 2

In the second part participants are asked to estimate the applied standard of a label. Here, they have to choose the level of the standard for different categories of environment friendliness. Those categories are about the fairness of the product (how fair the product is produced), the amount of emissions emitted and energy used during the production and if the use of resources and the consumption is sustainable. The last scale asks "How sure are you about your evaluation above?". The estimation is done on a scale from zero to 10, with zero meaning the lowest standard is applied and 10 being the highest. Additionally, we give participants another choice. If they think that a label does not consider a certain category they can choose "not included in standard". We included this option because some labels do not evaluate every aspect of environmental friendliness. Again, we present existing labels and phantasy labels. Participants can also choose the answers "I don't know this label."

3.3. Part 3

The third part of the experiment is to test the hypothesis of Harbaugh and colleagues that there are two equilibria coexisting. One is the labelling equilibrium, where all firms label and decide to show the label if they earned one and consumers expect a product to be labelled. In this first scenario, not having a label is like bad news for the consumers and, thus, decreases their willingness to pay. The second equilibrium is the non-labelling equilibrium. This case occurs, if not having a label is like nothing new to the consumers and, thus, does not have any impact on the willingness to pay. This scenario can be the case for products with a good reputation, for example Coca Cola, for which consumers simply do not expect a label or certificate. Then, firms will not label their product and rather save the labelling costs. In this task, participants see two pictures from the same product, one has a label on it the other does not have a label. We ask them, how much they would pay for each of the product. Additionally, we ask which of it they would prefer to buy, version A or B. In this task, we again include products with a phantasy label on it.

When they come to the last decision of this part, we offer them to claim information about the labels. This shows, whether participants are interested in knowing more about labels or not, even without an incentive.

3.4. The socio-demographic questionnaire

In this last part of the experiment, participants are asked fill in the questionnaire. It consists of some questions regarding their nationality, gender, age, education, hobbies and leisure activities, if they read the newspaper or are engaged in social activities and what they think the purpose of the experiment was. The last question is to elicit the experimenter demand effect. This effect occurs if participants try to do the *right* thing, more precisely what they think the experimenter wants them to do.

4. Data/ results

The result from part one should give us a first impression about how people estimate the product's quality only by seeing the it. The evaluation from this part shows if there are differences between labelled and unlabelled products. We test the difference for significance using a *t*-test. Here it could be interesting to see, if products labelled with fake labels still have a better reputation than label-free products. We are uncertain about expecting a higher or lower estimation of truthfully labelled products compared to unlabelled products. But if we are able to find significant differences between the three treatments this would be a confirmation of the opinion that labels are worth their costs and help increasing the reputation of a product.

In the second part we asked for the believes of the participants about the applied label standard. We presented existing, real labels and phantasy labels. We compare the evaluation of the real and the fake labels by, again, using a *t*-test for differences between the two variables. With this test we can find out how informed participants really are or if they are more or less always guessing when seeing a label. Further, we compare the participants estimates with the evaluation of a label expert to see if participants' believes are a good fit. The strength of how convinced participants are about their evaluation helps us to see the influence of a label in the next part of the experiment.

By asking about the willingness to pay and the preference for a labelled or unlabelled product in part three we can investigate two things. First, we can see if consumers generally prefer either labelled or unlabelled products. Additionally, we can test if the willingness to pay for a labelled product is significantly higher compared to the unlabelled product. If we can show that this is the case even for fake labels this would raise the question if the whole labelling process is beneficial in terms of consumer information. Consequently, each firm should get at least any label for the products and the Harbaugh-hypothesis about the coexistence of labelling and non-labelling equilibria could be rejected.

5. Conclusion/ Further research

Our experiment is a small approach of showing the effect of labels in general. Labels should work as a certificate for quality, increase the willingness to pay of the consumers and reduce the information asymmetries between the consumers and the firm. What we also investigate is if all labels have the power to increase the product evaluation, even the unreal labels. This would be worrying. Each firm could simply print a logo on their products which look similar like focal labels and thus they could benefit from a simple design choice. This then would be really confusing. The results from the second part shed light on the problem of what consumers really infer when they see a so far unknown label. If they really infer that the label only proves the lowest standard, the consequence must be that firms, the government and NGOs start to improve the reputation of the label and reduce this lack of information on the consumer's side. Interesting for this kind of action is the share of participants which choose to see some information. What is the solution to this information asymmetry problem if consumers are really not interested in what a label stands for? What if consumers only care that there is a label on the product and they can calm their queasy conscience? Another unanswered question is in the case of multiple equilibria, what determines which product needs a label and which has a good reputation speaking for itself?

An often-discussed topic is that labelling should be mandatory. This would solve at least the problem of multiple equilibria. The remaining equilibrium is that with labelling. But who is responsible for labelling? What happens with products from abroad? This experiment leaves a lot of questions unanswered. But it could show one thing: labels are an important tool in consumer information and relevant for the product evaluation. As one can see when walking through the supermarket, eco-friendly products have gained an enormous share and consumers are willing to pay more for sustainable and responsible products. But if labelling is not controlled and nearly everyone can create an own label this helpful tool can easily be misused and consumers pay the price.

6. Sources/ Literature

https://www.focus.de/kultur/vermischtes/groucho-marx-zum-40-todestag-die-besten-sprueche-von-groucho-marx_id_7490209.html

Harbaugh, R., Maxwell, J., Roussillon, B., Label Confusion: The Groucho Effect of Uncertain Standards, Management Science, Vol. 57, No. 9, 2011, pp. 1512-1527

YOUR KNOWLEDGE HAS VALUE

- We will publish your bachelor's and master's thesis, essays and papers

- Your own eBook and book - sold worldwide in all relevant shops

- Earn money with each sale

Upload your text at www.GRIN.com and publish for free